ENERGY
now and in the future

Solar Power

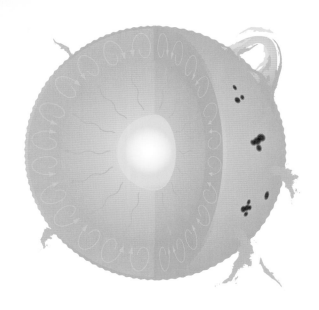

Neil Morris

FRANKLIN WATTS
LONDON • SYDNEY

ELIN

Z752483

An Appleseed Editions book

First published in 2009 by Franklin Watts
338 Euston Road, London NW1 3BH

Franklin Watts Australia
Hachette Children's Books
Level 17/207 Kent St, Sydney, NSW 2000

Created by Appleseed Editions Ltd,
Well House, Friars Hill, Guestling,
East Sussex TN35 4ET

Designed by Helen James
Edited by Mary-Jane Wilkins
Artwork by Guy Callaby
Picture research by Su Alexander

ISBN 978 0 7496 8774 8

Dewey Classification: 333.792'3

A CIP catalogue for this book is available from the British Library.

Photograph acknowledgements
page 9 Bettmann/Corbis; 10 Paul Hilton/epa/Corbis; 11 Robert Llewellyn/Corbis;
13 Keren Su/Corbis; 15 Science Photo Library; 17 Heinz Mollenhauer/Zefa/Corbis;
19 Keren Su/Corbis; 23 Ted Soqui/Corbis; 24 Nick Rains/Corbis; 25 Select Solar Ltd;
26 Roger Ressmeyer/Corbis; 28 George Steinmetz/Corbis; 31 Kendra Luck/San
Francisco Chronicle/Corbis; 32 Schlaich Bergermann and Partner, Stuttgart;
33 Peter Roggenthin/DPA/Corbis; 34 Paul Beckers/Nuon Solar Team;
36 Haruyoshi Yamaguchi/Corbis Sygma; 37 Regis Bossu/Sygma/Corbis;
38 NASA/Corbis; 39 Floris Leeuwenberg/The Cover Story/Corbis;
40 NASA; 43 White Design
Front cover Roger Ressmeyer/Corbis

Printed in China

Franklin Watts is a division of Hachette Children's Books,
an Hachette Livre UK company.
www.hachettelivre.co.uk

Contents

Energy from our local star

Have you ever wondered where all the world's energy comes from? That is, not just where it comes from when you flick on a light switch or fill up the car at a petrol station – but where the energy comes from originally?

The answer is that all our energy comes from the Sun, which makes the Sun the ultimate energy source. Solar power means 'power from the Sun', so you could say that all the world's different energy sources are really solar.

Burning star

The Sun is our very own star. Earth is one of its satellites, along with Mercury, Mars and the other planets. Our planet travels in an orbit around the Sun, making one complete journey every year. Like the other stars we see in the night sky, the Sun is a giant hot ball of burning gases. To us it looks different from the other stars because it is so much closer to us. The Sun's burning gases give off energy in the form of heat and make the star shine with its own light. All this energy is created by a process called nuclear fusion, which means the joining together of nuclei – the central parts of atoms.

Nuclear reactions take place in the central section of the Sun, called its core. This is the hottest section, with a temperature of 15,000,000°C. The core is so hot and dense that the nuclei of atoms of hydrogen – the lightest of all gases – join together to form the nucleus of a heavier gas, called helium. As they fuse, the nuclei give off enormous amounts of energy.

Energy on the move

The energy given off at the core travels towards the surface of the Sun in tiny particles called photons. These particles pass through layers of gas and bounce off other gas particles on the way. One individual photon might take more than a million years to pass through the Sun's inner, or radiative, zone.

At the top of the zone, the temperature is about 2,000,000°C. As they approach the surface and pass through the outer, convective zone, hotter photons rise and cooler photons fall.

At last photons reach the surface layer of the Sun, which is called the photosphere. The surface does not have a hard shell like the surface of the Earth, but is simply a mixture of glowing gases. The temperature here varies from about 6400°C at the bottom to about 4400°C at the top of the photosphere.

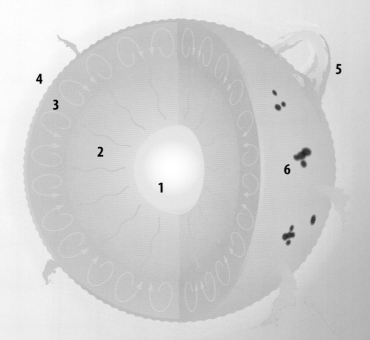

This cutaway illustration shows us inside the Sun, with its core in the centre. Photons travel all the way to the Sun's surface, a straight-line distance of nearly 700,000 kilometres.

1 Core
2 Radiative zone
3 Convective zone
4 Photosphere
5 Prominence
6 Sunspot

Will the Sun's energy ever run out?

Yes, it will, but not for a very long time. The Sun formed about 4.6 billion years ago and has used up about half of the hydrogen in its core so far. The nuclear reactions will continue and the Sun will keep shining steadily for another five billion years. That adds up to 50 million lifetimes, one after another, if each generation lived for 100 years. When the yellow Sun starts to run out of hydrogen, it will cool and swell up into a red giant star. Then the Earth will stop receiving solar energy.

Waves of energy

The Sun gives off most of its energy in the form of electromagnetic radiation – that is, electrical and magnetic waves of energy. Electromagnetic radiation is made up of a spectrum, or wide range, of different kinds of energy. From the waves with the least energy and longest wavelength to those with most energy and the shortest wavelength, they are:

- radio waves;
- microwaves;
- infrared rays;
- visible radiation (light);
- ultraviolet rays;
- X rays;
- gamma rays.

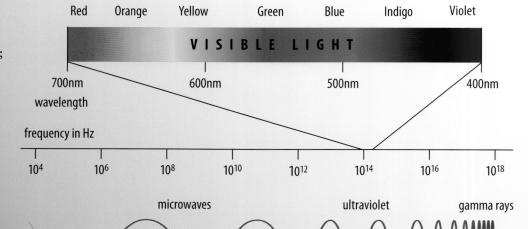

The electromagnetic spectrum. Visible light is split into its own spectrum of colours (shown at top).

What is a watt?

A watt (W) is a unit of power, which measures the rate of producing or using energy. The term was named after the Scottish engineer James Watt (1736-1819), who developed an improved steam engine. Watt himself measured his engine's performance in horsepower (hp). One horsepower equals 746 watts. Today, watts are generally used to measure electric power.

1 kilowatt (kW) = 1 thousand watts
1 megawatt (MW) = 1 million watts
1 gigawatt (GW) = 1 thousand million watts.

Nearly half of the Sun's electromagnetic radiation is in the form of infrared rays, which we feel on Earth as heat. Most of the other half is the visible radiation – or sunlight – to which our eyes are sensitive.

The blanket of gases that makes up the Earth's atmosphere blocks out about 60 per cent of all the Sun's radiation before it reaches us, including most of the high-energy ultraviolet, X and gamma rays. Without this blocking effect, these high-frequency, short-wave, high-energy rays would be harmful to us and to all living things on Earth.

The ultimate renewable resource

Solar power is called a renewable resource, because it is inexhaustible and we don't reduce stocks of it when we use it. In fact, we know that the Sun will eventually die (see page 7), but so far in the future that humans can forget about it for many millions of lifetimes.

Other energy sources – such as coal, oil and natural gas – are burned and used up to produce power. They are called non-renewable, because it takes millions of years for them to form underground. Solar power was what created these fossil fuels in the first place, so we can think of them as solar stores.

Some people think that energy research should concentrate on developing new ways of using solar power. Opponents to this way of thinking say that there are disadvantages to solar power, too. These include concerns about cost (see page 29), the use of land (see page 27) and whether it is practical to harness solar power in less sunny parts of the world (see page 17).

At the speed of light

The Sun's electromagnetic radiation travels out in all directions from the photosphere. All the radiation travels at the same speed – the fastest speed in the universe. We call it the speed of light. At nearly 300,000 kilometres per second, it is nearly a million times faster than the speed of sound on Earth (340 metres per second). This incredible speed means that solar radiation – or sunshine – shoots through 150 million kilometres of space to reach us on Earth in just over eight minutes. It takes more than four hours to reach the outermost planet, Neptune.

Astronauts communicate with each other by radio. The radio waves travel at the speed of light.

Making wind and weather

The Earth is a solar-powered planet. The Sun's radiation also creates the global weather system that allows the circulation of wind and water on Earth. Solar rays warm some parts of the world more than others, because some regions reflect the rays rather than absorbing them. This is known as the albedo effect. Snow and ice, for example, reflect up to 90 per cent of sunlight, while a sandy desert reflects half that amount, and oceans have an albedo of just 3.5 per cent.

On Earth, difference in temperature creates wind. Air above hot areas expands and rises, as air from cooler areas flows in to replace it. This movement of air is, of course, wind. This means that in the days when people used the wind to turn the sails of a windmill to grind grain, they were actually using solar power by means of the wind. The same is true when we use the blades of a modern wind turbine to generate electricity.

This modern wind farm makes electricity in southern China.

The water cycle

Solar energy also drives Earth's water cycle. The Sun's rays heat the world's oceans, making water change into a gas called water vapour. The light vapour rises into the air, where it cools and forms tiny droplets of water that join to make clouds. Eventually the water falls back to Earth as rain.

On land, much of the rain flows into streams and rivers, which take the water back to the ocean. There the endless water cycle starts all over again. So when we use the power of moving water to produce electricity – whether through hydroelectric dams, tidal barrages or wave devices – once again we are actually using solar power by means of the water cycle.

Plants and the Sun

The world's plants use visible radiation, or light energy, to make their own food. They do this by the process of photosynthesis, which means 'putting together with light'. Plants capture sunlight and use it to combine water and minerals from the soil with carbon dioxide gas from the air and convert them into chemical energy. During this process plants give off oxygen, which we and all animals need to breathe and stay alive. So when we use the power of biomass – plant and animal matter – to produce energy or electricity, we are using solar power by means of photosynthesis.

Trees and all other plants depend on the Sun's rays to drive the process of photosynthesis.

The greenhouse effect and global warming

The atmosphere prevents some of the Sun's rays from reaching Earth. Its gases also stop some heat escaping from Earth, just as glass traps warmth inside a greenhouse. We add to this natural greenhouse effect by emitting waste (or greenhouse gases) from power plants, factories and cars. We produce many of these greenhouse gases — especially carbon dioxide — when we burn coal, oil or gas to release energy. Experts have discovered that in this way humans are increasing the effects of natural climate change and making it more extreme. The way we use energy is adding to global warming, so that land, sea and air temperatures are gradually increasing. This is a great concern because global warming is melting ice sheets so that sea levels are rising. It is also creating more heatwaves, droughts and severe weather.

The significance of the Sun

Long before humans knew that the Sun was a star that provided us with all our heat and light, our ancestors worshipped the yellow ball in the sky as a life-giving force.

Many cultures gave particular importance to gods and goddesses of the Sun. In ancient Egypt there were several. The greatest of these was Re, who was thought to be the visible body, and especially the eye, of the lord of heaven. From about 2600 BC, Re was worshipped at a cult centre called Iunu, which came to be known by the Greek name Heliopolis – Sun City.

Wonder of the world

The ancient Greek Sun god was called Helios. Every day he drove a chariot from east to west across the sky. Every night Helios sailed around the northerly stream of the ocean in a golden cup. This Sun deity was especially worshipped in Rhodes, where he became the chief god. To give thanks for protecting them against invaders, the islanders of Rhodes built a giant statue of Helios at the entrance to their harbour in 280 BC. The statue became known as the Colossus of Rhodes, and it was one of the original Seven Wonders of the Ancient World.

Re joined Herakhty (or Horus, the sky god) as the rising Sun in the morning. The Sun god spent the day crossing the heavens, which the Egyptians saw as an ocean, in his solar boat. When the evening arrived and the Sun set, Re became associated with the creator god Atum. By about 2500 BC, Egyptians regarded the Sun god as their chief deity. From then on, they gave their pharaoh, or king, the ultimate title, Son of Re.

Gods, emperors and kings

Many other cultures associated their rulers with a Sun god, in the same way as the Egyptians. The ancient Japanese religion of Shinto had a Sun goddess named Amaterasu. She was considered the supreme ruler of the world. Until the mid-twentieth century, Japanese people worshipped their emperor as a direct descendant of

Amaterasu-Omikami, or the great divinity illuminating heaven. Japan is still known as the land of the rising Sun, and this symbol is on the national flag.

Among the Inca people of Peru, the emperor (or Inca) was an incarnation of the Sun god Inti. This god was seen as the original ancestor of all the people. The Inca were known as the children of the Sun, and they eventually founded their own city, Cuzco, the capital of the Inca empire.

The unconquered Sun

The ancient Romans worshipped Sol, and around AD 220 the Sun god came to be known as Sol Invictus (the unconquered Sun). Every year the Romans celebrated the winter solstice – the shortest day when the Sun is lowest in the sky. This also marked the birthday of the unconquered Sun, on 25 December. Early Christians made that day their Christmas festival.

Modern Peruvians put on ceremonial dress to celebrate a traditional Inca festival of the Sun.

Early solar heating

People have used the heat of the Sun – passive solar heating – since ancient times. The city of Priene (in modern Turkey) was first settled by Ionians in the eleventh century BC. When they rebuilt the city 700 years later, the Ionians laid out the city in a rectangle on a slope running down to the sea. The main streets ran from east to west and all the buildings faced south. This allowed the Sun to warm the houses during the winter. The north side of each house was designed to be closed and sheltered, to keep out the cold winter winds.

The great ancient Greek philosophers Aristotle and Socrates both advised city planners and builders to lay out their houses this way. In the fifth century BC the playwright Aeschylus stated that only primitive barbarians would be stupid enough not to build their houses to face the Sun.

Around the first century AD the ancient Romans added glass to windows, so that rooms acted as solar heat traps. They had a special room called a heliocaminus (or sun furnace) in public baths and other buildings, which was circular with a domed roof. This room was similar to a conservatory or solarium today. The Romans even passed laws to prevent builders blocking other people's light and heat.

Scientific advances

In 1515 the Italian artist and scientist Leonardo da Vinci drew designs for a large curved mirror. His plan was to use the reflective surface to focus the Sun's rays on to a boiler, so heating water to dye cloth.

By the eighteenth century, scientists were using glass to concentrate light and heat things. In 1772, the French chemist Antoine Lavoisier used a series of large glass lenses to melt metals and even to burn diamond. He then discovered that diamond gave off a gas that

Antoine Lavoisier (1743-94) built this device to hold large glass lenses and focus the Sun's rays. Friends were invited to watch his experiments in combustion.

we now know as carbon dioxide (because diamond is made of carbon). Most importantly, he found that combustion took place best in a gas that he named oxygen.

In 1839, French physicist Alexandre-Edmond Becquerel found that electricity passed between two metal plates when one was exposed to sunlight. This led to the invention of the solar cell (see pages 20-21).

A nineteenth-century solar motor

As early as the mid-nineteeth century, many Europeans were becoming concerned about stocks of coal — the great energy source that had become more important than wood. In 1860 a French mathematics teacher named Augustin Mouchot (1823-1912) started work on a solar motor. This was a cauldron of water enclosed in glass, which was placed in sunlight. When the water boiled, it produced steam which ran a small engine. Emperor Napoleon III was so impressed that he sent Mouchot to sunny Algeria in north Africa to continue his work. But coal prices in France dropped and put an end to the mathematician's solar developments.

Harnessing the Sun's energy

One of the best and easiest ways to make direct use of the Sun's energy is to install solar panels as part of a hot-water system. The flat panels are positioned on a roof, facing the right direction (south in the northern hemisphere) and tilted to the best angle to collect as much sunshine as possible.

Each solar panel is made of metal, often painted black to absorb the most heat (because of the albedo effect, see page 10). The panel has a glass cover on top and a series of narrow pipes running through it. The pipes are warmed by the Sun's heat, which is then absorbed by the water or other liquid inside them.

The glass cover allows the Sun's rays through, but traps a layer of warm air to keep the panel warm (because of the greenhouse effect, see page 11). This means that the panel can produce hot, or at least warm, water even in cooler air temperatures. The liquid in the panel is moved through a closed loop of pipes by an electric pump, which uses very little power.

Depending on the strength of the Sun's rays, the system can collect more than ten times as much solar power as the amount of electrical power taken to run the pump. Some systems use a photovoltaic

1 Solar rays

2 Solar panel

3 Pump

4 Heat exchanger

5 Hot water tank

6 Expansion vessel

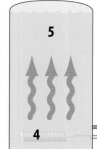
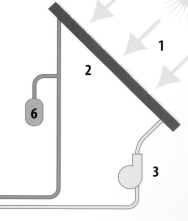

This diagram shows how a simple solar thermal system heats water.

panel (see page 20) to generate electricity to run the pump, so that they are completely solar-powered.

Solar panels on a roof can run a complete hot-water system.

As the water in the system is heated and cooled, it expands and contracts. To keep the pressure in the system constant, there is an expansion vessel to allow for changes in water volume. The heated water from the solar panel is moved to the hot-water tank, which has a heat exchanger inside – usually a heat-transfer coil in the bottom of the tank.

This thermal system is called an active, indirect system (see page 18). It is very efficient at transferring heat. The closed system contains antifreeze to protect the pipes from damage in cold weather. The whole system can be run by an electronic controller which uses sensors to work out when the panel is hotter than the water in the tank, so it knows when to switch the pump on and off.

Do solar thermal systems only work in hot regions?

Solar hot-water systems do work better in hot countries, but they are also useful in cooler regions, such as northern Europe and North America. Modern hot-water tanks with solar-heating coils are very efficient and only slightly more expensive than an ordinary tank.

On days with little sunshine, the system can be backed up by a boiler powered by gas or another fuel. The backup boiler has less work to do and uses less energy, as the water has been pre-heated by the solar thermal system.

Four different systems

There are four different kinds of solar thermal systems, called active, passive, direct and indirect.

• An active system needs electric power to work a pump and the controls.
• A passive system uses convection to circulate the water. Some passive systems have a storage tank above the solar panel; others place the storage tank inside the collector.
• A direct system heats drinkable water directly in the collector.
• An indirect system heats a fluid, such as propylene glycol, and transfers heat to drinkable water using a heat exchanger.

How people use solar thermal systems

Solar thermal systems produce hot water for homes, which accounts for a large part of many people's energy bills. Another popular use in cooler climates is to heat swimming pools. In hot climates, the system is not really necessary, because sunshine warms the pool water naturally.

A solar thermal system for a swimming pool can be the same system as for hot water. But as swimming pools already have a pump and filter system to move the water around, it's more efficient to fit a special system to this.

Is it worth the bother?

Many people are beginning to realize that it's important to look after the environment and one way to do this is to use as little energy as possible. A solar thermal system is an advantage in an eco-friendly house. Hot water is important for hygiene, and everybody uses energy to produce it.

In Britain and other countries, people who want to sell their homes now have to declare how energy efficient they are. Thermal systems cost quite a lot to install, but many countries offer grants to help set them up. A system should pay for itself in under ten years, and DIY enthusiasts can fit thermal systems themselves. You might think swimming pools are only for very rich people, but if they can be heated and run cheaply, they will have wider appeal.

Some new thermal systems don't even have fixed glass panels. Specialist companies make what they call solar matting, from a synthetic resin called PVC (polyvinyl chloride). The black mats contain small pipes, through which the water is pumped to heat it. The matting can be put on a roof, garage, pool house or even on a nearby lawn. You need about half the surface area of the pool in PVC matting, which is quite a lot. This system works well because it uses the pump which is already there, and it can be controlled so that water only goes through the thermal panels or mats when the pool water drops to a certain temperature.

Heating water for cooking

In some parts of the developing world, people use reflectors rather than panels to heat water directly. Curved pieces of shiny metal reflect sunlight on to a small area, where a metal ring holds a pot or kettle. It works very well!

This Chinese solar cooker
is being used to boil water.

Sunlight in cells

Photovoltaic systems convert solar energy into electricity, using sunlight to power electrical equipment. The term photovoltaic comes from photo (meaning light) and volt (a unit of electrical force). So photovoltaic power means 'electrical power from light' – which of course comes from the Sun.

Scientists first made photovoltaic (or solar) cells during the nineteeth century, but they were not very efficient until the 1950s. Then scientists found ways to make the cells much more powerful. Photovoltaic (PV) cells work by the movement of electrons, which are particles that occur in atoms.

Panels and batteries

The electrical output from a single PV cell is quite small, so cells are connected to each other behind a glass cover to form a module (usually called a panel). Modules can be fitted together to cover a large area, such as a roof. Just as a hot-water tank can store the heat from a thermal panel, batteries can store the electricity

Do PV systems need bright sunshine?

PV cells generate more electricity on bright days than when skies are overcast. But even on overcast days a PV cell generates some electricity, because photovoltaics do not need to be in direct sunlight to work. In other words, the brighter the sunshine, the more electricity a PV cell produces. In regions with less sunshine, a PV system might need backup from other energy sources (just like solar thermal systems with gas-fired backup, see page 17).

HOW A PHOTOVOLTAIC CELL WORKS

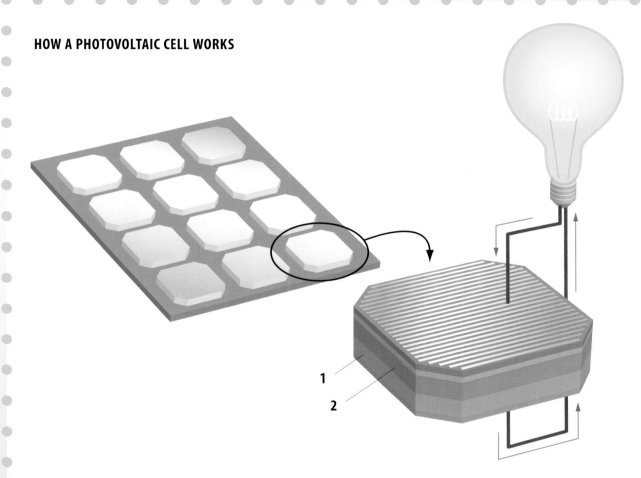

Photovoltaic cells are made up of two separate layers of a chemical element (usually silicon) which are placed under a glass cover. One of the layers is treated with a chemical to make a p (or positive) layer (1), and the other is treated differently to make an n (or negative) layer (2).

When sunlight hits the solar cell, the p, or positive, layer loses electrons and the n, or negative, layer collects them. This makes the electrons pass between the metal contacts at the front and back of the cell which creates the flow of an electric current within the cell.

from a PV panel. This is useful, because the PV panels can produce more electricity than is needed immediately.

A solar light needs a rechargeable battery, which collects electricity from a PV panel during the hours of daylight, and stores it until it is needed to power the lightbulb when it becomes dark.

Solar power around the world

Today, the world's hottest countries do not produce the most electricity from photovoltaic sources. Germany is the world leader and just five countries use almost all the electriticity generated in this way.

WHO USES THE MOST SOLAR POWER?	
Country	% of world PV use
Germany	49.9
Japan	29.8
USA	10.9
Spain	2.1
Australia	1.2
Total	**93.9%**

WORLD ANNUAL PV MARKET (MW)

2000	2001	2002	2003	2004	2005	2006
278	334	439	594	1052	1320	1467

Although Germany comes top of the league, the electricity it generates from photovoltaic sources is still only 0.3 per cent of all the electricity it produces. This is much less than it produces from other renewable sources, such as wind turbines and hydroelectric projects.

Some of the world's largest PV installations are in Germany, for example Erlasee Solar Park in Bavaria. There, 1500 groups of solar panels cover an area of 77 hectares (about the same as 100 football pitches). This array produces enough electricity for the nearby town of Arnstein, which has a population of more than 8000.

High-rise solar power

In Japan, PV panels are being built into modern high-rise office buildings, such as the headquarters of the Kyocera company in the city of Kyoto. The 18-storey Kyocera building has 504 solar panels on its roof and another 1392 panels on the south-facing side of the building. If the building used an oil-powered plant to produce the same amount of electricity, it would burn 32,000 litres of oil a year.

The Los Angeles Caltrans (California Department of Transportation) District 7 building, completed in 2004, has movable PV cells. The architects were given a design award by the US Green Building Council.

Another building with solar panels is the 13-storey Caltrans District 7 Headquarters, in Los Angeles. The building's south side has PV panels that rise and fall as the sunlight hits them, to make them as efficient as possible. This makes the building look as though it is always moving. Environmentalists like the building, but the *LA Downtown News* reports that others call it an 'ominous grey structure', and a 'futuristic fortress'.

Supporting solar power

In Spain, all new and renovated houses must have solar panels. Owners are given financial help to install them. Germany and other countries offer grants which aim to encourage people to set up systems using solar power. People can also sell any electricity they produce but do not need to the national grid (see page 42).

Making the environment a priority

The environmental organization Greenpeace says that solar panels could be used to supply much more electricity. It says: 'Solarizing your home is one way you can become your own electricity producer and help to protect our world from the devastating effects of climate change.' However, many people are put off by the cost of installing a solar system. Environmentalists say that governments should contribute more through grants and that in most countries people are not paid a fair price for electricity they generate. Customers have to pay much more for electricity from the national grid than they receive for any they sell.

A solar-powered telephone booth in a small settlement in South Australia. This is a practical use of PV technology in a sunny part of the world.

Solar power in developing countries

In poorer parts of the world, many people have no mains electricity. Solar power can be very useful here. But solar panels are expensive to buy so many people cannot afford to install them. A good example is the southern African country of Namibia. There, a German company runs a fleet of mobile solar units, which supply electricity to small settlements. Solar-powered and wind-powered base stations are also used to run a mobile phone network in Namibia. The electricity is stored in large underground batteries. Water pumps are also run by photovoltaic power.

Powering calculators

One of the earliest uses of small-scale PV cells was to power pocket calculators. They have no batteries, so there has to be a light source for the calculator to work. If you are working at your desk and there is not enough sunlight to power the calculator, you just have to switch on an electric light. It will work straight away.

Energy to run gadgets and toys

Many companies use PV technology to power gadgets, including phones, torches and even power tools. Most use rechargeable batteries to store the energy they make, and there are even solar-powered battery chargers. Toy manufacturers sell robot toys operated by solar cells. One ingenious gadget is a solar-powered fan, so people can use sunshine to create a cool breeze. You can even buy a solar-powered fan built into a sun hat or baseball cap.

Do solar cells cause pollution?

PV energy is very popular with environmentalists because solar cells do not give off gases or anything that could harm the environment or enhance the greenhouse effect. However, Greenpeace and other environmental organizations are concerned that poisonous chemicals are used to manufacture PV cells.

There are different kinds of cells and some use a poisonous metallic element called cadmium. This is also used in some rechargeable batteries. But according to the environmental publisher Earthscan, coal-fired power stations emit 360 times more cadmium into the air to generate the same amount of electricity as a solar cell. In 2007, a British research project announced a new way of manufacturing solar cells which causes no environmental problems.

Using sunshine in clothing

Did you know that there are solar bikinis? The bikini has tiny strips of photovoltaic film sewn into it with special thread. A simple connection means that it can be used to power a mobile phone or MP3 player. A new development for clothing is the infrared solar cell. This reacts to the Sun's rays in the infrared part of the spectrum (see page 8) rather than visible light. Researchers believe that small infrared cells could be sewn into clothing, or even sprayed on to it, to provide people with electricity on the move.

How about a solar-powered fan in the peak of your cap? 'Cool caps' could be just the thing for tropical travellers.

Concentrating solar power

Research programmes have shown that solar energy could power large plants which generate electricity by placing large banks of photovoltaic cells next to each other.

But future electricity power plants may use concentrating solar power (CSP) systems to generate large quantities of electricity. One CSP system uses reflecting dishes called parabolic reflectors. These concentrate sunlight on to a receiver which contains a fluid that is heated. The receiver contains a heat engine that generates electricity.

Scientists are also developing new methods for the hotter regions of the world, where the Sun's power is greater and can be heightened even more.

Power from the desert?

The Trans-Mediterranean Renewable Energy Cooperation (TREC) is a network of scientists and experts in renewable energy which aims to generate power from deserts. Its researchers believe that we could generate enough electricity for the whole world in a 300-kilometre-square region of hot desert. This area is shown on the map opposite as part of Algeria, taking up just four per cent of the country's total area.

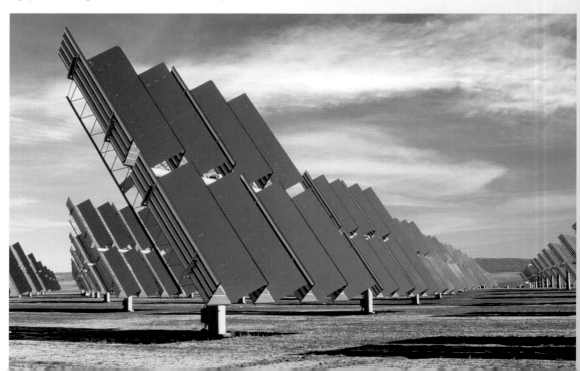

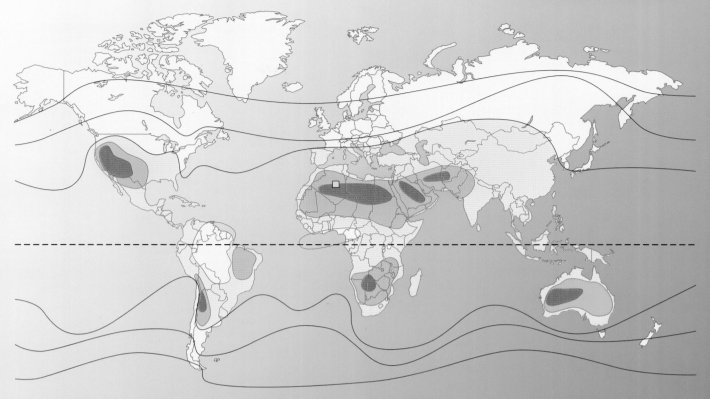

TREC also believes that waste heat from the generated power can be used to desalinate seawater. After driving electricity generators, the heat from a solar plant in the form of steam could be piped through tanks of seawater. The seawater would boil and evaporate to leave fresh water.

The organization believes that solar power plants in the northern regions of the Sahara Desert could generate enough electricity and desalinated seawater to supply the whole of Europe, the Middle East and North Africa. The scheme would take up less than 0.3 per cent of the desert areas of the region. Researchers in Australia, where more than a fifth of the land is desert, are also working on Desertec (desert technology) projects.

Opposite: panels at a solar power plant in California, USA (in the red, excellent zone of the world).

The red areas are excellent locations for solar power plants. The orange areas are good, yellow are suitable, and blue regions are possible. The square in North Africa is the area mentioned on page 26.

Do we have enough spare land?

One of the disadvantages of large-scale solar power schemes is that they need enormous amounts of land to house the collectors and reflectors. This would not be a problem in desert regions, where most land cannot be used in other ways.

Solar plants take up less space than hydroelectric dams or coal-fired power stations when you compare the amount of electricity generated with the total size of the plant. That's if you include the size of reservoirs for dams and mines for coal in the calculations for hydroelectric and coal-fired power stations.

Solar One and Two

Experimental CSP plants have been built since the 1980s, and the technology is improving. A plant called Solar One opened in the Mojave Desert of California in 1982, with more than 1800 heliostats. It used water as the heating fluid, and ran until 1986.

Then more than a hundred large heliostats were added and the plant was developed into Solar Two, using molten salt instead of water. This plant generated 10 MW (megawatts) of electricity from 1995 to 2001. These projects showed that the technology worked, and the US Department of Energy's solar initiative aims to make solar energy competitive with other sources by 2015.

Some of the heliostats and the tower of Solar Two. The plant covered more than 82,000 square metres at Daggett, in the Mojave Desert of southern California.

Concentrating the Sun's rays

Some concentrating solar power (CSP) plants have a large array of mirrors, called heliostats, which reflect and focus sunlight on to a tall tower. There the concentrated sunlight heats a fluid in a receiver, creating temperatures up to 3000°C. Scientists are trying out various fluids for this purpose, including liquid sodium, which stores heat very well. The heat in the receiver boils water, which produces steam and drives a turbine connected to an electric generator.

Spanish power tower

In 2007 a new CSP plant opened near Seville, in sunny southern Spain. The PS10 plant has 624 movable heliostats that reflect sunlight on to its 115-metre high tower.

But what happens when the Sun sets? The PS10 plant has four large tanks where heat can be stored in molten salt so the turbine can keep working at night. At this stage, the plant generates 11 MW of electricity. This is enough to power up to 6000 homes. There are plans to build more CSP plants in the area, which will generate a total of 300 MW by 2013.

Will it cost too much?

Most experts believe that the cost of producing CSP electricity is up to three times higher than producing electricity from traditional sources such as fossil fuels. But they also point out that costs will fall as the technology develops and is used on a larger scale. These costs do not take environmental issues into account. Clearing up pollution and developing projects to counteract global warming also cost a great deal of money.

But not everyone is convinced about the future of solar power. British environmentalist James Lovelock, who developed the Gaia Theory (which treats the Earth as a living organism), is not enthusiastic. In his book *The Revenge of Gaia* (2006), Lovelock writes: 'As with wind, the intermittency of solar supply would necessitate efficient energy storage, and so far this too is unavailable. I find it hard to believe that large-scale solar energy plants in desert regions, where the intensity and constancy of sunlight could be relied on, would compare in cost and reliability with fission and fusion energy, especially when the cost of transmitting the energy was taken into account.'

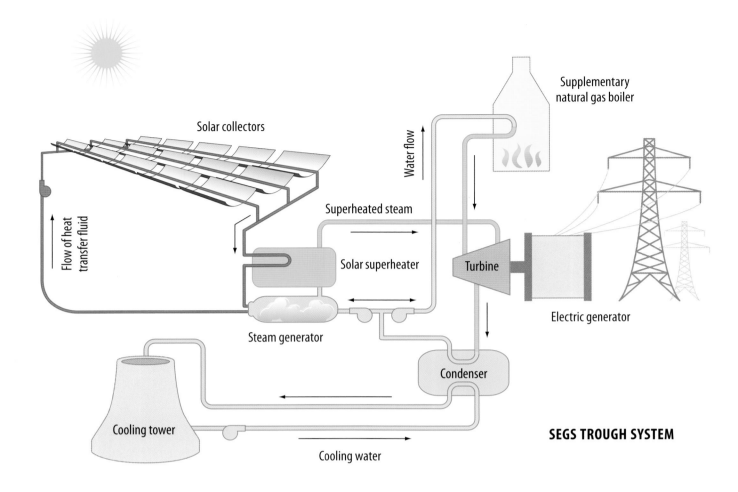

Solar collectors

Supplementary natural gas boiler

Water flow

Flow of heat transfer fluid

Superheated steam

Solar superheater

Turbine

Electric generator

Steam generator

Condenser

Cooling tower

Cooling water

SEGS TROUGH SYSTEM

Different shaped reflectors

Sunlight can be reflected and concentrated by curved, trough-shaped reflectors on to a thin steel receiver pipe running along the inside of the curved surface. This heats oil (called a heat transfer fluid) that flows through the pipe.

The reflectors are computer-controlled to move slightly during the course of the day, tracking the sun from east to west so that maximum sunlight is collected and directed at the receiver pipes. The hot oil passes to a heat exchanger, where it boils water to produce steam. As in other systems, the steam turns the blades of a turbine connected to a generator that produces electricity.

Most powerful in the world

Solar Energy Generating Systems (SEGS) form a series of nine solar power plants at Daggett, Harper Lake and Kramer Junction in California's Mojave Desert. The plants started operating between 1984 and 1991, and all use the solar trough system.

The troughs are made up of more than 900,000 reflectors, and the installations cover more than 9 sq km of desert. SEGS VIII and IX each generate 80 MW, which makes them the most powerful solar power plants in the world. Together, the SEGS plants provide enough electricity for 230,000 homes. They have a gas-fired boiler to back up the system when there is not enough sunshine.

Opposite: how the solar energy generating system works, with solar collectors heating a fluid that creates steam to drive a turbine.

Combined systems

One of the problems with solar systems is storage during night-time and in the winter. Storage systems are expensive, so most experiments have used something called a hybrid system. This involves using a solar system in combination with a gas-fired or other fossil fuel plant, which is used when solar electricity is not being produced.

Further research

Solar research is going on all the time. While some scientists are convinced by one system or another, many believe we need further research to find the best, most efficient system. In the Tabernas desert, near Almeria in southern Spain, there is a research establishment called Plataforma Solar de Almeria (PSA) that compares systems such as power towers and parabolic troughs.

'Not in my back yard!'

How would you set about trying to convince people that they should use green electricity, and especially solar electricity? Do people really care, or do they simply want the cheapest electricity they can buy?

Perhaps one way to convince people might be to give them the facts about how their electricity is produced. Do you feel more positive about solar energy now that you know a bit more about it? Do you think consumers might feel differently if they were given this information?

One of the problems is that people do not want unsightly buildings to be visible from their living-room window. This is known as a NIMBY (Not In My Back Yard) attitude. People are happy to have solar panels or even power stations, but they always want them somewhere else.

Rows of reflecting troughs in a California solar power plant.

SOLAR POWER

Solar power towers

A solar updraft tower works on the basic principle that hot air rises. The tower is surrounded by a large plastic greenhouse, which is open at the ends to let in cool air. The air is warmed by the Sun and moves towards the centre and the tower, so that it can rise. As the air moves through the tower, it turns the blades of one or more wind turbines, which are connected to an electric generator.

Early projects

In 1982, a prototype of a solar updraft power plant was built by a German engineer in Manzanares, Spain. The tower was 195 metres tall and 10 metres wide, surrounded by a greenhouse (or collection area) about 250 metres in diameter. This pilot project ran until 1989 and produced electricity successfully, although engineers became worried about the stability and strength of the tower in strong winds. There are proposals to build another tower in Spain which will be

The experimental solar updraft tower in Spain. It was built and tested by a German engineering company in cooperation with the Spanish government. The tower proved that this system can work.

These solar panels stand on the site of a former waste dump near Nuremberg, in southern Germany. This is a good use of a south-facing hillside, but some people might say that the panels spoil the landscape.

much taller – 750 metres high. The greenhouse area will cover an area about 3.5 sq km.

Another huge scheme called the Solar Mission Project is under way in Australia. SMP's tower will be 1000 metres tall, making it the tallest structure in the world. It will be 120 metres wide and surrounded by a 100 sq km greenhouse, where the air will be heated to 43°C more than normal. The air will move at more than 50 km/h and drive 32 turbines around the bottom of the tower. Although the turbines are at the bottom, the height of the tower is important, because this creates the wind. The electricity output is expected to power 200,000 homes.

The company building the tower believes this massive project will change the way people think about solar power and green electricity. They plan to build more towers. Most importantly, they know from earlier prototypes that the plant will be able to run 24 hours a day. That's because at night the ground releases heat it has stored during the day, which keeps the air moving and the turbines turning.

Will these solar plants really work?

You might think that these are research projects rather than reliable large-scale power plants. But the technology is changing fast. According to David Howell and Carole Nakhle in their book *Out of the Energy Labyrinth* (Tauris, 2007), 'It is conceivable that solar power could yet be "the next big thing". The technology has been described as "about where mobile phones were ten years ago".' If so, there may be amazing developments just around the corner. As usual, the real question is money. Big projects need big investment, so governments and large companies need to be involved.

Sun-powered travel

There has been a lot of research into finding ways of using the Sun's energy to power vehicles. Inventors and creative engineers have come up with ways of harnessing solar power directly to drive cars, boats and even planes.

Many adventurous experiments have been successful.

They have concentrated on using photovoltaic cells to power electric motors that turn wheels or propellers.

World Solar Challenge

In 1982 the Danish-born inventor and environmentalist Hans Thostrup drove the world's first solar-powered car Quiet Achiever all the way across Australia, from Perth in the west to Sydney in the east. The car took 20 days to cover more than 4000 km, at an average speed of 23 km/h. Thostrup's success encouraged him to set a challenge to other engineers – to race 3000 km across the Australian desert, from Darwin in the north

Nuna 4 (with race number 3) won the World Solar Challenge in 2007. Its Dutch student engineers say it has a top speed of at least 142 km/h.

to Adelaide in the south. The first World Solar Challenge took place in 1987 and was won by Sunraycer, sponsored by General Motors, at an average speed of 67 km/h.

Dutch success

The World Solar Challenge now takes place every two years. The last four races have been won by solar cars called Nuna, built by technology students at Delft University in the Netherlands. In 2005 Nuna 3 won the race at a record average speed of 103 km/h. The organizers of the race were concerned that the solar cars were travelling faster than the Australian speed limit, and in 2007 they brought in new rules. These included reducing the area of the solar panels from nine to six sq m. Nuna 4 won the 2007 Challenge at a speed of 91 km/h.

NUNA 4 SPECIFICATIONS 2007	
Length	4.72 m
Weight	187 kg
Wheels	3
Solar cells	2318
Max speed	142 km/h
Battery	30 kg
Body	mainly carbon fibre

Like all solar vehicles, sun-powered cars have large arrays of PV cells in a horizontal position, to catch as much sunlight as possible. They also have large batteries, which store the electricity so that the cars can go on running when there is little sunshine. During the World Solar Challenge, the cars race all day and stop at night. The batteries are heavy, slowing the cars down, so engineers have to work out carefully how big to make them.

Could we use solar cars as everyday vehicles?

Solar cars are not yet practical, for a number of reasons. The array of solar cells takes up a large area, so is difficult to design into an ordinary road car. Also, solar cars need a large battery (or series of batteries), which is not very practical. Nevertheless, some car companies are working on building a solar array into a hybrid car, such as the Toyota Prius. Hybrids have a petrol engine but use an electric motor to run the car at low speeds. The battery for the motor is recharged by the action of the brakes. It could also be recharged by solar cells.

Ships powered by sunshine

The first solar-powered boats appeared in the 1970s, and used PV cells to drive their propellers. In 1996 the Japanese sailor Kenichi Horie crossed the Pacific Ocean in a solar-powered boat. In 2007 a Swiss-built, 14-metre long solar catamaran called Sun21 crossed the Atlantic Ocean from Rotterdam to New York. The catamaran kept up a speed of about 11 km/h all the way, day and night, using batteries to store electricity.

There are plans to develop and build a solar-powered craft that can sail around the world. The largest solar boat yet built is the 27-metre Solarshuttle, which carries up to 100 tourists on the River Alster in Germany.

Solar wings

In 2001, an experimental solar unmanned aerial vehicle (UAV) set a world record for a propeller-driven aircraft by reaching a height of 29,524 metres. The UAV was built by NASA and named Helios, after the Greek Sun god. It was really a flying wing, with 14 propellers powered by more than 60,000 solar cells spread across

Space satellites and rovers

Solar cells work well in space, where there are no clouds or seasons. Drum-shaped satellites have solar cells all the way round, providing electricity to power their computers, cameras and communications. Larger spacecraft have flat panels that stick out like wings and turn to face the Sun at the best angle. In 2004, two rover vehicles travelled on Mars, which is about 78 million kilometres further away from the Sun than Earth (so sunlight takes four minutes longer to reach it). The rovers were sent to a region near the Martian equator, so they received enough sunlight. They worked perfectly.

Opposite: Kenichi Horie arrives in Tokyo in his aluminium solar-powered boat. His voyage across the Pacific from Ecuador took 148 days.

Aren't solar boats and planes just for fun?

Attempts at solar flight and sailing are adventurous experiments, but that is how many technological developments have begun. Many sailors believe that solar power can work commercially for boats and even larger ships. According to *National Geographic* magazine, 'If solar-powered planes prove successful, they would have many practical applications. This is especially true given their renewable energy source and theoretical ability for continuous flight. Commercial applications could include using solar planes as telecommunications platforms, which would be capable of dispersing broadband media over wide areas. As suborbital satellites, the high-flying planes could potentially be used for military reconnaissance and monitoring weather and other natural phenomena.'

the top. In 2007, a British lightweight solar aircraft named Zephyr broke the record for the longest unmanned flight by staying up for 54 hours.

Plans are being made to fly around the world under solar power. The Swiss balloonist Bertrand Piccard is part of a team planning to start test flights on Solar Impulse in 2009. Piccard says, 'It will need to be very light and use very little energy at night. Energy storage is the biggest challenge for solar flight.' The plane will have a 61-metre wingspan and will be able to generate enough power to fly at nearly 100 km/h.

A solar-powered plane makes a test flight. There are several such aircraft in development.

What does the future hold?

The use of solar power as an energy source is growing all the time. This growth is driven by many different groups of people.

Scientists and engineers are constantly looking for new ways to use our ultimate energy source. Politicians want to be able to convince voters that their future energy requirements will be met and that there are not going to be shortages of fuel or electricity. Environmentalists are concerned that energy policies do not increase environmental pollution or contribute further to global warming. Meanwhile, large and small-scale projects continue to show the whole community how important, useful and effective solar power can be.

Out in space

The International Space Station (ISS) is a research facility that has been assembled in space since 1998. The station, which orbits the Earth 15 times a day, is a joint project between the United States,

The International Space Station is powered by solar 'wings'.

Russia, Japan, Canada and the 17 member countries of the European Space Agency. Astronauts have lived aboard the station since 2000, replacing each other regularly.

The station's electricity comes from its large array of solar panels. These are 58 metres long and cover an area of about 4000 square metres. The panels turn towards the Sun as the station orbits Earth. In 2007, one of the PV panels was damaged while it was being repositioned. Space-shuttle astronauts managed to repair it manually – an amazing achievement.

This 15m diameter solar collector in Auroville, southern India, powers the boiler in a kitchen below. The solar kitchen can cook two meals a day for 1000 people.

Helping the developing world

On a much smaller scale on Earth, solar panels can be very helpful in the developing world (see page 24). As well as lighting and heating homes, the panels can be used to power radios and recharge mobile phones and laptop computers.

About a million people live in the poverty-stricken Kibera district of Nairobi (the capital of Kenya). In 2007 a project called the Kibera Community Youth Programme (KCYP) won a World Clean Energy Award for its work with simple, small and affordable solar panels. Young people from the district have been taught to assemble the solar panels, which are cheap to buy. The programme has increased the availability and understanding of solar power throughout Kenya and neighbouring countries.

How much should we spend?

Scientific development projects need huge sums of money to keep going. Space programmes are expensive, and many Americans are not convinced that the sums spent by NASA are worthwhile. However, when they realize that the programmes have practical advantages, they may feel differently.

Governments in Germany, Japan and other countries have invested heavily in solar power by offering incentives which encourage people to install solar panels. People can apply for financial help with the initial cost and tax benefits to help them afford solar systems. If all developed countries did this, solar power would have a greater chance of development.

SOLAR POWER

Sun towers in space

Many new solar techniques are on the drawing board. In the United States, NASA is working on technology called space-based solar power (SSP).

Technicians want to put giant man-made solar cells into space. A double row of 32 cells would form a sun tower that would never be affected by cloud cover or the cycle of day and night. This means that it would receive eight times as much sunlight as similar cells on Earth. The energy collected in space would be sent as microwave radiation to Earth, where antennae would capture it and turn it into electricity. This new technology could be available by 2020.

Solar cities

The International Solar Energy Society (ISES) works to support the science of solar energy and research to show how it can be helpful here on Earth. One of its programmes is called the Solar Cities Initiative, which aims to look at the best ways to use energy in the 'habitats of tomorrow'. Scientists at ISES are particularly interested in cities as complete systems in themselves, where solar power could provide most energy.

This NASA image shows what space engineers expect their sun tower to look like.

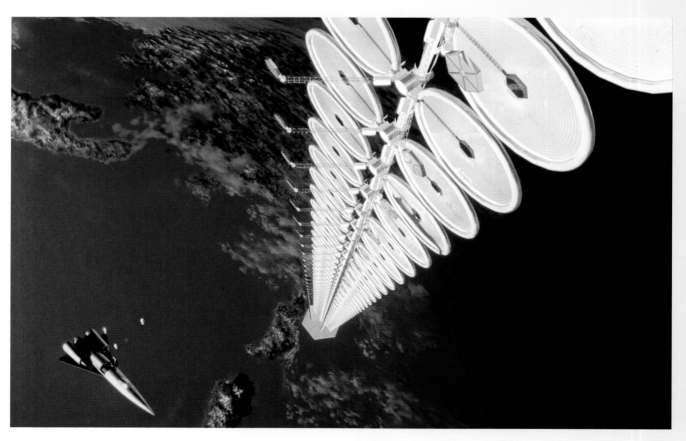

Another SSP idea is to set up power-generating stations on the moon. Lunar power bases could supply Earth via microwaves. If there were bases on opposite sides of the moon, they could send a constant stream of electrical energy to antennae on Earth.

Solar sail

A solar sail catches sunlight in the same way as a ship's sails catch the wind. The idea behind the solar sail was first proposed by the German astronomer Johannes Kepler (1571-1630), but it is only being put into practice now. The sail is actually a membrane mirror, which is made of a very light, reflective material, such as aluminium film. It reflects sunlight and, as it does so, particles of solar energy provide a tiny amount of thrust and push the sail through space. A sail can be used to propel spacecraft and could have other uses in future.

The science of solar sails is well understood, but the technology of their use needs further development. In 2005 an unmanned spacecraft called Cosmos 1 attempted to travel through space using a solar sail, but its launch rocket failed.

Do all scientists agree?

Scientists do not all agree on the importance or future of solar energy. Most believe that it is useful, but some agree with James Lovelock (see page 29) that solar power is a sensible energy supplement rather than a primary source.

However, the director of the Centre for Energy Policy and Technology writes in the magazine *Physics World*: 'Over vast areas of the developing world, the incident solar energy is 2000-2700 kWh per square metre of ground occupied per year. Solar-thermal power stations can convert more than 20 per cent of this to electricity, and photovoltaics now on the market about 15 per cent of it... All of the world's future energy demands could, in theory, be met by solar devices occupying about one per cent of the land now used for crops and pasture, or the same area of land currently inundated by hydroelectric schemes.'

SOLAR POWER

The solar house of the future?

The European Photovoltaic Industry Association believes that PV power could provide energy for more than one billion people by 2020. The association also says it could provide at least one fifth of our global electricity needs by 2040. One of the ways to achieve this would be to convince people in the developed world to convert to PV living.

The best solution is for a house to have its own PV solar panels, but also be connected to the mains electricity grid. As shown below, the house needs an inverter to change PV-generated electricity from direct into alternating current. When more electricity is produced than needed, it goes to the grid. When the house does not have enough solar power, it imports electricity from the grid. The meter checks how much electricity passes each way and at the end of every quarter sends either a bill or a credit to the householder.

SOLAR HOUSE

1 PV solar panels
2 Junction box
3 Inverter
4 Import/export meter
5 Connector to grid

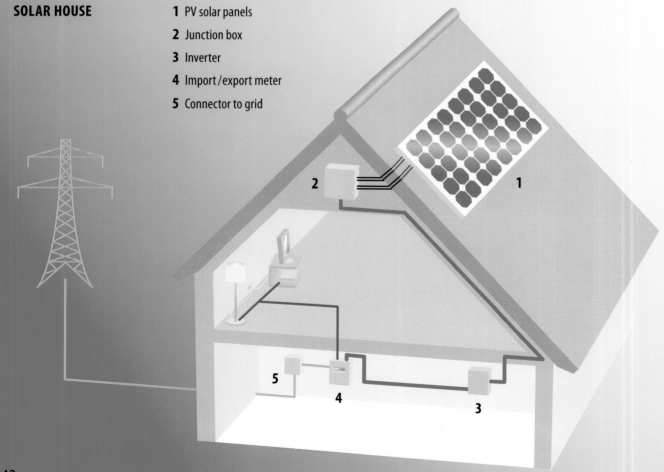

In some countries, such as Germany and Spain, the government encourages this system by making the electricity companies pay a higher price for solar electricity than they charge for conventional electricity.

This school in north-west England has both PV and thermal solar panels for heating and lighting. Its students benefit from solar power as they learn about its use.

Bringing down costs

Whatever the future holds for solar power, one thing is certain: cost will be of utmost importance. The outlook for solar costs looks good, and this may tip the balance in its favour if all other problems can be overcome. Many experts are positive about future solar power. In his book *Global Warming: the Complete Briefing* (2004), the physicist and climate change expert John Houghton writes: 'In the short term, increased development of local [solar] installations is likely to have priority; later, with the expectation of a significant cost reduction... large-scale electricity generation will become more possible. Eventually, because of its simplicity, convenience and cleanliness... electricity from solar PV sources will become one of the largest... of the world's energy sources.'

ELIN	
Z752483	
PETERS	27-Feb-2012
333.7923	£12.99

Should solar power be part of the energy mix?

Given the problems and disadvantages, should we look at solar power as the sole solution to our energy needs for the future? Many experts believe it would be much better to view solar power as one element in an energy mix of renewable resources (solar, wind, water, geothermal and biomass) and non-renewable sources (fossil fuels and nuclear energy). That way we can avoid the possibility of an energy gap. The solar house shown is a good individual example, mixing solar with other sources depending on requirements.

Glossary

albedo effect   The capacity of a substance to reflect the Sun's rays rather than absorb them; snow and ice are highly reflective and so have a high albedo.

atom   The basic particle of all matter.

biomass   All plant and animal matter, especially when used as a fuel.

cadmium   A soft bluish-white metallic element.

carbon dioxide (CO_2)   A greenhouse gas given off when fossil fuels are burned.

climate change   A change in general weather conditions over a long period of time, including higher temperatures, more or less rain, drought, etc.

convective zone   The region below the surface of the Sun where hotter photons rise and cooler photons sink.

desalinate   To remove the salt from seawater.

electromagnetic spectrum   The range of electrical and magnetic radiation given off by the Sun, which includes radio waves and visible light.

electron   A negatively charged particle within an atom.

energy efficient   Using energy sensibly and without waste.

expansion vessel   A container in a heating system that allows the volume of water to expand (or increase).

fossil fuel   A fuel (such as coal, oil and natural gas) that comes from the remains of prehistoric plants and animals.

Gaia theory   The idea that the Earth is a self-regulating organism (or living thing).

gamma rays   High-energy rays given off by nuclear reactions.

global warming   Heating up of the Earth's surface, especially caused by pollution from burning fossil fuels.

greenhouse gas   A gas, such as carbon dioxide, that traps heat from the Sun near the Earth and helps to create the greenhouse effect.

heat exchanger   A device that transfers heat from one substance to another.

heliostat   A movable mirror that reflects sunlight.

helium   A non-flammable colourless gas.

hybrid   A system made up of different elements, such as a power system using solar and gas energy.

hydrogen   A light, colourless gas that combines with oxygen to make water.

incentive   Something that encourages somebody to do something.

infrared rays   Electromagnetic rays with a wavelength greater than visible light rays.

membrane A thin sheet.

non-renewable resources Resources (such as fossil fuels) that are used up and cannot be replaced.

nucleus The central part of an atom.

oxygen A colourless gas that humans and animals need to breathe to live.

parabolic reflector A curved surface that reflects the Sun's rays on to a collector.

photon A particle of electromagnetic radiation.

photosphere The Sun's outer layer of gas.

propylene glycol A liquid alcohol that is used in antifreeze and heating systems.

PVC (polyvinyl chloride) A hard-wearing plastic substance.

red giant A large, red-coloured star.

renewable resources Sources of energy that do not run out, such as biomass, geothermal, solar, water and wind power.

silicon A chemical element found in sand and many minerals.

sodium A soft metallic chemical element.

turbine A machine with rotating blades that turn a shaft.

ultraviolet rays Electromagnetic rays with a shorter wavelength than visible light rays.

X rays High-energy rays between ultraviolet and gamma rays on the electromagnetic spectrum.

Websites

BBC features on solar power and installing solar panels

www.bbc.co.uk/nature/animals/features/324feature1.shtml

www.bbc.co.uk/climate/adaptation/solar_power.shtml

The International Solar Energy Society – a global alliance

www.ises.org

An interesting history of solar power

www.solarenergy.com/info_history.html

Some fascinating facts about solar power

www.solel.com/faq/

Index